DEVELOPING TEACHING

TEACHING MORE STUDENTS

1

PROBLEMS AND COURSE DESIGN STRATEGIES

Graham Gibbs

Design Team:

Elizabeth Beaty, David Baume

Consultant Team:

Gina Wisker, Chris Rust, David McAndrew, Alan Jenkins, David Jaques, Trevor Habeshaw, Graham Gibbs, Bob Farmer, Diana Eastcott, Sally Brown, Elizabeth Beaty, David Baume

The TEACHING MORE STUDENTS Project

The aim of the project is to offer lecturers and course leaders support in facing the challenge of increased student numbers and larger classes. It will be difficult to maintain quality in learning if course design, teaching and assessment methods remain unchanged. To support change, the project will deliver about 100 training workshops in Polytechnics and Colleges throughout England to about 3,000 academic staff. The workshops will be delivered in most institutions during 1992.

The workshops will be tailored to meet the needs of each institution, based on the following workshop modules:

1 Teaching more students: problems and strategic options
2 Lecturing to more students
3 Discussion with more students
4 Assessing more students
5 Independent learning with more students
6 Course design for teaching more students

The workshops will support lecturers by:

- identifying the nature of teaching and learning problems encountered with increasing student numbers
- offering a range of alternative strategies and methods, based on best practice, which can be used to address these problems
- illustrating and demonstrating these methods
- assisting lecturers to select the most appropriate methods for their contexts, and to plan their implementation
- providing resource material to support follow-up work

The project will be delivered by a team of experienced educational development consultants from eight Polytechnics and Colleges, managed by the Oxford Centre for Staff Development under the direction of Graham Gibbs. The impact of the workshops on participants' teaching and on institutions will be evaluated.

For further information contact:
The Oxford Centre for Staff Development
Oxford Brookes University
Oxford OX3 0BP
Tel 0865 750918
FAX 0865 744437

The TEACHING MORE STUDENTS Project
is funded by the Polytechnics and Colleges Funding Council

Contents

Workshop aims

By the end of the workshop participants will have:

- identified the main areas of problems their students face in large classes;
- examined broad strategic options for addressing these problems;
- identified the most promising options for their own contexts.

1 Students' experience of courses with more students

"I found some of the large classes overwhelming. The size of this place and the number of people was totally overwhelming."

"It's hard to get to know people. In the lectures there is just a sea of faces you don't even recognise, let alone know."

"I don't know who is running this course - it's certainly not the tutor we get for our seminars and it's a different lecturer practically every week. I'd like to meet the mastermind behind all this!"

"It's so full. The corridors are full. The refectory is full. The library is full. The classrooms are absolutely packed out. There is nowhere to park. There isn't even anywhere to sit quietly and get on with your studying."

"I mean they were standing on people's heads, they were. He initially told half of them to get out and return next term, and we were in the first week of arriving. It was jam-packed. Absolutely amazing. That's happened in quite a few of mine."

"It's hard to tell if you are on the right track. You get so little feedback. You could be going in the wrong directions. By the time you get your work back you've taken the exam and failed."

"It's chaos, but just manageable because there is the structure of the workbook. Without that people would panic."

"The books are just out. It's not suprising with God knows how many of us after the same books. Even if you think you've got to the library before anyone else they are still out. Well they may not be out, because there is a lot of hiding going on - people putting books where only they can find them."

"The lectures are OK - there are about 80 of us - as long as you aren't at the back. You can't see or hear from the back. God knows what it is like in the Main Hall with 400-odd."

"You can tell they haven't marked your work properly. It's just a few ticks and scribbles. It's depressing after all the work you put into it but I don't really blame them. - - - needed two people to help him carry the essays away last time."

"I think there are about 26 seminar groups. You sometimes wonder if we are all getting the same course!"

2 Data on student numbers and class sizes

The patterns of teaching and learning common in British higher education were established in times when class sizes were rather different from what they are today. The *Robbins Report* (1963) included data on class size. It reported that lectures were given, on average, to 28 students, though to far fewer in the humanities, and that final-year lectures were given, on average, to 18 students. A third of all lectures were given to under 10 students. No less than 73% of all tutorials were one-to-one. In science a large practical class was considered to be more than 10.

The data below, in contrast, are from the Modular Course at Oxford Polytechnic. This is a large modular degree programme made up of about 1,000 one-term modules in 1992. The table shows how the number of large classes has risen over a five-year period. These data were collected before the sharp increases in student numbers of the early 1990s.

No. of students attending the module	No. of modules of different size 1984/85	1989/90	% increase over 5 years
0 - 60	545	680	25%
61 - 100	64	118	84%
101 - 180	22	69	214%
181 - 400	0	10	∞

Proportionately the largest increases have been in the larger class sizes and it is in the area of the largest classes that the Polytechnic can accommodate (180 - 400) that growth has been fastest. These increases in class sizes are larger than the increases in overall student numbers on the Modular Course. This effect is the result of a modular course structure and the need to cope with very large numbers on introductory courses in the first year. Throughout higher education it seems that increases in the number of large classes are running well ahead of increases in student numbers.

The Government has outlined plans to increase student numbers in higher education by a further 60% or so during the remainder of the decade.

Reference

"Students and their Education", *Robbins Report*. London: HMSO, 1963, Appendix 2 (B)

3 Problems faced by lecturers and students

Any changes made in course design should directly address problems which arise from accommodating more students. The grid overleaf is for you to record your perceptions of problems relating to lectures, discussion, assessment, independent learning and any other areas, such as laboratory teaching, on one course with which you are familiar. Problems lecturers perceive are not always the same as those experienced by students. You are invited to distinguish between problems for lecturers and for students for each aspect of the course.

Aspect of course	Problems for lecturers	Problems for students
Lectures		
Discussion groups		
Assessment		
Independent learning		
Other areas		

4 Learning problems with more students

Method	What has happened	Resulting problems
Lectures	Classes much larger	Difficult for students to ask questions
		Difficult for lecturers to know if students understand
		Difficult to elicit student answers
		Due to lack of other contact, lecture notes need to be self-contained and complete, which encourages dictation
		Difficult to encourage interaction between students
	Lecture rooms bigger	Heightened problems of acoustics, visibility and attention
Seminars	Groups much bigger	Students do not know each other
		Tutor does not know the students
		Easy for students to "hide" and not take part
		Difficult for tutor to respond to individuals
		Low student participation
		Little opportunity for individuals to pursue interests
		Participation dominated by tutor and a few students
		Poor preparation due to inadequate library provision
		High absenteeism tolerated or not noticed
	Less frequent meetings	Students continue not to know each other
		Lack of group cohesion and momentum
		Poor links with lectures and coursework

Method	What has happened	Resulting problems
		As there is more material to be dealt with, discussion is superficial or very selective
	Multiple seminar groups & multiple tutors	Lack of consistency of content
		Quality control poor
		Stale, bored tutors
		Scheduling problems
Reading	Fewer books per student in the library	Less reading, less relevant reading, patchy reading in the library
	Students unable to afford books	Narrower focus, particularly in lectures and seminars which aim to "cover" ground the textbooks cover
	Narrower range of books	Narrower, predictable reading; predictable essays
	Single copy of reference material (e.g. journals, law reports)	Journals become unrealistic source for students
	Library space limited	Reading discouraged
	Study space limited	Overcrowded coffee lounges used for reading
Essays and assignments	Fewer and less frequent	Less practice at writing
		Less preparation for exams
		Smaller proportion of course material studied in depth
		Encourages "selective negligence"
		Students put in fewer learning hours
		Lack of momentum and pacing to study
		Being rarer, essays become more anxiety-provoking
	Overstretched tutors require shorter assignments	Students develop different skills
		Less emphasis on collating evidence into coherent arguments

Method	What has happened	Resulting problems
	Less feedback	Less learning
		Less improvement in essay-writing
Laboratories	Class size larger	Less hands-on experience
		Experience of only part of a procedure
		Less supervision
		Labs often more limited and routine
	Lab splits/repeats	Scheduling and timing problems in relation to programme of lectures
		Stale, bored tutors
	Tutors require shorter and fewer reports	Less feedback on skill
		Fewer links between theory and practice
		Writing skills not developed
	More routine labs	Experimental design skills not developed
		Students bored
Practical work	Too little equipment	Familiarity with equipment limited
	Fewer field trips	Theory not linked with experience
	Less time with equipment	Insufficient practice
Creative work	Less supervision and guidance	Students develop more slowly and waste effort
	Less time in the studio	Less hands-on experience, or more isolated learning
	Crowded studios	Uncongenial learning environment
	Shared studios	No personalised learning space
		Time wasted setting up and removing work
Supervised project and dissertation work	Less negotiation and clarification of project	Lack of direction and sense of ownership of project
	Less supervision and encouragement	Less focussed and productive student effort
	Limited access to resources	Narrower, shallower projects and frustrated students

Method	What has happened	Resulting problems
Problem classes	Less feedback on work in progress	Less development of skills
	Larger classes	Less individual time with tutors
		More time wasted while "stuck"
	Fewer classes	Less continuity and progression
		Skills not reinforced, leading to problems later
One-to-one tutorials	Fewer and shorter	Insufficient diagnosis of learning difficulties
		Insufficient "modelling" of academic reasoning and problem-solving
		Lack of interaction and discussion in student learning
	Tutors harder to contact	Students unable to progress and lose motivation
		Serious student problems not picked up in time

If you use other teaching methods you will find it helpful to analyse the effects of larger student numbers on their effectiveness.

Other methods	What has happened	Resulting problems

The problems arising from increased student numbers may be summarised in eight categories.

4.1 Courses lack clear aims and objectives

It is insufficiently clear to students what a course consists of: what is to be learnt, what is the purpose of specific assignments or reading, what an acceptable outcome of learning would look like. Conventional courses achieve a degree of clarity of purpose not through design, but through informal face-to-face contact. When this is reduced to a minimum, students lose direction. Lectures have never worked well to clarify purpose and the trend to return to lecturing as a way of coping with large numbers has only highlighted the difficulty.

4.2 Students lack knowledge about their progress

Students need to know how they are doing: whether they are working hard enough, understand things adequately and are generally keeping up. As the number of assignments and tutorials drops and tutor feedback declines, so students lose this crucial sense of how they are doing. There is a much greater chance of them getting seriously behind or of progressing while unaware of serious flaws in their understanding or competence. This tends to lead to higher failure and drop-out rates and a good deal of anguish.

4.3 Students lack advice on how to improve

Even if students know they are not doing as well as expected, they still need to know what to do about it - how to improve. In large classes if students receive any advice it tends to be rather general in nature, addressed to the whole class, concerning the most common problems. There is a lack of individualised, specific help.

4.4 Library resources cannot support wide reading

Conventional courses require extensive library resources. 200 students being required to "read around" this week's topic stretches libraries well beyond their ability to cope. As a result students read less, and less widely.

4.5 Tutors are unable to support independent study

Traditional project and dissertation work involves one-to-one tutorial support and individual practical or laboratory work. This is becoming increasingly difficult to sustain and students are frequently left for long periods without adequate guidance and assistance.

4.6 Students lack the opportunity for discussion

In large classes student learning is becoming solitary. The negotiation of meaning and exploration of half-formed ideas, which discussion offers, is being denied to students.

4.7 Tutors are unable to cope with the variety of students

At a time when the variety of student backgrounds has never been wider, the ability of tutors to respond flexibly to students through personal contact has been taken away. Students are being treated as a homogeneous mass.

4.8 Tutors are unable to motivate students

In the past motivation came from personal contact with lecturers and involvement in small-group discussion. When students' imagination was fired, library and other resources were available to support exploration and new thinking. In large classes, in the absence of either personal contact or small groups, and with inadequate resources to fuel motivation, students are frequently disengaged and passive.

5 Control and independence strategies

There are two highly contrasting sets of strategies for dealing with these difficulties. One is to control the situation - a strategy popular in undergraduate classes in North America - and the other is to foster students' freedom and independence. The best way to explain this difference is to examine the methods adopted by these two strategies for tackling each of the eight problem areas outlined in Section 4. The methods listed in the table are explained in more detail below.

Problem areas resulting from large classes	Characteristic methods adopted	
	Control strategies	**Independence strategies**
1 Courses lack clear aims and objectives	Use of objectives	Use of learning contracts
	Highly structured courses	Problem-based learning
2 Students lack knowledge about their progress	Objective testing	Development of student judgement
	Programmed instruction and CAL	Self-assessment
3 Students lack advice on how to improve	Assignment attachment forms	Peer feedback and peer-assessment
	Automated tutorial feedback	
4 Library resources cannot support wide reading	Use of set books	Development of students' research skills
	Use of learning packages	More varied assignments
5 Tutors are unable to support independent study	Structured projects	Group work
	Lab guides	Learning teams
6 Students lack the opportunity for discussion	Structured lectures	Student-led seminars
	Structured seminars and workshops	Team assignments
7 Tutors are unable to cope with the variety of students	Pre-tests plus remedial material	Variety of support mechanisms
	Self-paced study	Negotiated goals
8 Tutors are unable to motivate students	Frequent testing	Learning contracts, problem-solving, group work
	High failure rates	

Problem 1:

Control strategies

Control strategies involve the teacher defining the purpose of courses, classes and assignments in advance, in some detail, and in designing learning activities so that they tie in very closely with these pre-defined purposes.

Use of objectives

Objectives are statements of what should have been achieved on completion of a course of study. Behavioural objectives state these achievements in terms of the behaviour you would want to be able to observe in your students; for example:

> At the end of this section readers should be able to:
> (a) list and describe the main problems encountered in large classes;
> (b) list the main features of "control" and "independence" strategies for dealing with problems in large classes;
> (c) describe and contrast different methods associated with these strategies.

This clearly provides much more information for the student than would a syllabus listing. When objectives also provide a strong framework for assessment they make it very explicit what is to be learnt.

Behavioural objectives became very widely used in the USA in the 1950s and '60s; they are still the basis of much course design and, in particular, objective testing such as the use of multiple choice questions. Objectives were adopted by the Open University in the 1970s for distance learning, to clarify course goals in the absence of contact between teacher and student, and to guide the writing of "CMAs" (computer-marked assignments). Formal statements of objectives are still a central feature of course design in B/TEC courses. B/TEC have their own typology of levels of objectives and link the proportion of objectives at each level to the level of the course and the types of assessment methods used. They are used to standardise courses and control quality.

Highly structured courses

The purpose of a particular section of a course can be clarified by its function in relation to other sections of the course. Courses can be designed with considerable attention to the prerequisite knowledge needed, knowledge required for subsequent sections, logical ordering of material, remedial attention necessary at each stage, and so on. Multiple choice testing may be used to make decisions about what element of this structure the student is directed to next. This kind of approach to course design is most appropriate to subject matter which has its own logical structure involving clear sequences of prerequisites.

Courses lack clear aims and objectives

Independence strategies

Independence strategies involve students specifying their own purposes in personally relevant ways, or setting the tackling and solving of problems as the goal instead of more abstract specifications of learning outcomes.

Use of learning contracts

Learning contracts are agreements between teachers and students about learning. They can involve statements about what is to be learnt, what resources will be used, what steps will be taken in order to achieve the desired outcomes, what the outcomes will look like and how they will be assessed. They are normally negotiated between teachers and students in order to give a clear purpose to independent studying. Learning contracts can be very extensive, involving an entire qualification (as with the Diploma in Higher Education by Independent Study at Suffolk College) or quite modest, involving a few days' work experience. Learning contracts can provide a framework within which students can supervise their own independent learning, confident of their goals.

Problem-based learning

Problem-based learning provides problems to be tackled, through which learning takes place. For the learner the purpose of the activity is clear even if the learning outcomes are not yet obvious. People seem to have a natural propensity for tackling problems and find them inherently engaging. In some forms of problem-based learning there is a detailed analysis of the knowledge base the problem draws upon, to guide learners, and most problem-based learning also involves groups who help to give direction to learning.

Problem 2:

Control strategies

Control strategies involve testing students by asking questions to which the teacher has the correct answer, and informing them whether they are correct or not.

Objective testing

The commonest form of objective testing is the multiple choice question test, though there are other question formats that allow students to record their answers in a way which can be quickly and objectively marked. The ease of marking allows frequent and extensive testing, and the use of computers, either with optical mark readers (OMRs) or screen-based systems, increases the speed and ease still further. The installation of a computer-marking system at Oxford Polytechnic has led to a wide range of applications, within subjects such as Education and Economics as well as science and technology subjects.

Programmed instruction and computer-assisted learning (CAL)

Programmed instruction and its applications with computers require the learner to work through a long series of very short tutorial steps. Each step involves some input of material followed by a test of that material. Students are directed to the next step or to remedial material depending on their response. This is the ultimate level of control that can be exerted over student learning - each minute step is under the control of the designer of the programme. More flexible types of tutorial programme have been developed for computer-assisted learning, and it has been greatly enlivened by colour, graphics, moving images, touch screens, sound and even interaction with video, audio or CD. However, programmed learning remains a control strategy.

Students lack knowledge about their progress

Independence strategies

Independence strategies involve developing students' ability to recognise their own progress and judge their own work, even to the point of awarding themselves grades.

Development of student judgement

When tutors take all the responsibility for marking, students often hand in work for assessment without even reading it. Students have little idea what mark it might get or why. Academics do not rely entirely on others for a sense of the quality of their work - they make their own judgements and re-draft and improve their own work. If students are to monitor their own performance and correct their own work they need to develop their criteria and judgement about what constitutes quality in academic work. They need to undertake marking exercises, see other students' work, and discuss what is good and bad about a variety of assignments.

Self-assessment

One very effective way of developing students' judgement is to require them to write self-assessment comments on their own work before they submit it, on a self-assessment sheet. Such sheets can include questions such as the following:

> What are the best features of your assignment?
> How could your assignment be improved?
> What would you have to do to get one grade higher than the grade you are going to get?

Students need to develop a sense of when they have done enough on a topic and when they can move on to the next task - they need to assess their own progress and achievements.

Problem 3:

Control strategies

Control strategies consist of mechanising feedback. They use criteria, and sometimes even feedback, which are fixed to the course rather than responsive to the individual.

Assignment attachment forms

Assignment attachment forms are used by tutors to give structured feedback to students on their written work. They usually involve a list of criteria and rating scales and tutors tick boxes on the scales to give students feedback.

Automated tutorial feedback

Multiple choice question testing based on computers can have tutorial comments attached to each incorrect response so that students get back not just a print-out of their test score but a tutorial comment for each incorrect answer given. These tutorial comments are written at the same time as the tests. It is possible to use computer-marked tests not to allocate marks but purely for feedback to students, and questions and their tutorial comments can be written with this feedback role in mind.

Students lack advice on how to improve

Independence strategies

Independence strategies involve using students to give feedback to each other, either informally or through formal assessment processes.

Peer feedback and peer-assessment

Students are perfectly capable of giving useful feedback on one another's work. Indeed, it can be very effective to require students to obtain feedback on an essay or lab report, and to show how they have responded to this feedback in the final draft which is submitted for assessment. In technical areas it is easy to give students marking schemes to mark one another's work. Studies have shown that peers can be very reliable, and monitoring for collusion is relatively straightforward. In some situations, such as in seminar work or group project work, peers are in the best position to give feedback and even to allocate marks, and a range of workable techniques exist to ensure fairness.

Problem 4:

Control strategies

Control strategies consist of specifying set readings and providing these in full for all students.

Use of set books

Many undergraduate courses in North America, and most in the first year, use a set textbook. Use of textbooks can guarantee that students have access to core material but may also make it likely that they do not go far beyond this core material. Many American textbooks come with sets of multiple choice test questions, study guides and even tutor guides, so that whole courses can be built around them with little extra design work.

Use of learning packages

Learning packages can provide students with much of the reading material they need and refer them to any additional sources. They may also include questions about the reading and short tasks. In elaborate forms they may resemble distance-learning materials such as Open University course units. In this form the packages often attempt to control minute details of students' learning from moment to moment by taking them through material in a logical step-by-step manner with questions and answers interspersed with the text.

Library resources cannot support wide reading

Independence strategies

Independence strategies involve widening the range of relevant sources so that students are not all chasing the same material at once. This implies wider varieties of assignments and also the development of students' ability to locate and use a wider variety of information sources.

Development of students' research skills

An example of this strategy is a first-year Sociology course, described in Jenkins and Gibbs (1992), in which resources are allocated in the first term to enable students to develop the research skills necessary to cope with less support in the second and third terms. The course is supported by a workbook containing a series of library search exercises, some of which are assessed. Students provided with textbooks and learning packages containing all the necessary reading can become dependent on such support and do not develop the necessary research skills. With library resources so stretched, students very often find that the recommended book is out. With research skills they can cope with this problem in a variety of ways.

More varied assignments

One way of getting round the problem of 200 students chasing the same sources is to invent more varied assignments which draw on a wider range of sources both within the library and outside. For example, a Business Law programme at Wolverhampton Polytechnic involves teams of students going to business libraries, the Department of Trade and Industry, and to a range of the kinds of information sources which lawyers actually use. This requires more independence, of course, but with sufficient thought and support even first-year students need not be restricted in their reading.

Problem 5:

Control strategies

Control strategies consist of narrowing and controlling the range of student independent study through specifying purposes, activities, resources, steps to be taken, etc. until study resembles following instructions.

Structured projects

It is possible to enable even large numbers of students to undertake complex independent projects with little face-to-face support if the written guidance is comprehensive enough. It might need to include a schedule of tasks, deadlines and instructions for meetings with other students, a good bibliography and notes on sources, direct advice on what not to do, checklists, data-analysis forms, advice on writing the project report, criteria for marking the project and so on.

Lab guides

Lab guides can contain all the instructions students need to undertake an experiment, use a piece of equipment or analyse results. Guides can contain diagrams of equipment, whole sections of lab reports ready written, data-recording sheets, graphs with the axes already correctly labelled, and so on. While it is possible for a lab guide to substitute for a considerable amount of the face-to-face support students would otherwise have obtained from tutors or demonstrators, it may leave students with little to do but follow instructions. As a result such guides have become known as "recipe books". However, it is possible to be selective about which aspects of the lab to support with written material, leaving students to focus on one aspect of the lab independently each week; for example, the experimental design, setting up the equipment, error estimation or interpreting the data.

Tutors are unable to support independent study

Independence strategies

Independence strategies tend to involve the use of students to "supervise" and support each other, through group projects and learning teams, and also the use of learning contracts as a framework within which such support can be provided.

Group work

Students can tackle more complex, more extensive and more open-ended projects if they work in groups. Instead of relying on one-to-one supervision, tutors need only supervise the group. And if attention is paid to developing group-work skills the group can become very effective at managing itself and supervising its members. Students can learn how to run independent tutor-less seminar groups. Project teams can be set up to undertake independent fieldwork and research. Laboratory groups can be set up to design, run and write up practical experimentation. Assessment methods are available to allocate marks to individuals within groups when the group submits a single product for assessment.

Learning teams

A case study in Jenkins and Gibbs (1992) describes how learning teams were set up on a large part-time BA Business Studies course to support the independent study of mature students. There was very little contact with tutors but the learning teams provided peer tuition and support. Learning teams can share reading material and lecture notes, comment on each other's essays, provide "personal tutoring", revise together and generally support each other's learning.

Problem 6:

Control strategies

Control strategies consist of introducing discussion of teacher-set questions and tasks in fixed time slots within teacher-directed sessions.

Structured lectures

In large lecture classes it is impossible to bring about open, unstructured discussion but it is possible to introduce short discussion activities for pairs or threes (see Booklet 2: *Lecturing to More Students* for examples). It requires very clear instructions, strict time-keeping and a firm hand for regaining control in order to continue the lecture, but it can be done. A considerable degree of control needs to be exerted to cope with very large numbers. Such discussions are inevitably limited in scope.

Structured seminars and workshops

As seminar groups grow to above ten or so, unstructured discussions become less satisfactory and the majority of students present will not participate to any great extent. However, a wide range of structures can be used to encourage active participation, such as rounds, pyramids, line-ups, pairs, syndicates and brainstorming (see Booklet 3: *Discussion with More Students* for examples). Pyramids, for example, involve students working on their own, then in pairs, then in fours, and finally as a whole class. By building up to open discussion in this way students develop their ideas and their confidence and are more likely to contribute productively even when the class is as large as 30. All these methods, however effective at getting students to join in, involve control of the class and of the topics being discussed.

Students lack the opportunity for discussion

Independence strategies

Independence strategies make use of students' ability to hold discussions on their own, either through formal student-led seminars, or through co-operative work on assignments.

Student-led seminars

Students can run their own seminar groups without a tutor present. At Oxford Polytechnic, Education students take turns, in pairs, to lead a seminar session. They give a presentation, provide handouts and follow-up references and lead a discussion. As they are assessed by the rest of their group they take this responsibility seriously and make sure the session is engaging and well run. Other, parallel, groups are working in the same way. The tutor tours the groups to make sure they are OK. There is not usually much work for the tutor to do!

Team assignments

Students can learn to co-operate on assignments and projects, laboratory work, fieldwork, seminar presentations and even reading assignments. This can generate a great deal of discussion outside the class. The assessment requirements and the design of classroom sessions are powerful tools to influence the ways in which students study independently.

Problem 7:

Control strategies

Control strategies consist of controlling entry and progress so that only those students who pass teacher-set tests can proceed. They are well suited to structured curricula in Mathematics and the sciences where prerequisite knowledge can be specified clearly.

Pre-tests plus remedial material

Highly structured courses with clear objectives often specify the level of knowledge or competence expected on entry. It is possible to set entry tests, or "pre-tests", to check on students' prior knowledge. You can then either turn away unsuitable students, referring them to a more suitable, lower-level course, or offer remedial material so that they can catch up in their own time in parallel with the course. This remedial material can be computer-based or in independent learning packages in the library, and may make no demands on the tutors at all. Such remedial material would typically include self-tests so that students can check for themselves when they have reached an acceptable standard in relation to the entry level for the course.

Self-paced study

This involves allowing students to progress as fast as they are able or as slowly as they need. It usually requires clearly stated objectives and a course divided into self-contained units, each with its own objectives and objective tests. In the "Keller Plan" or "Personalised System of Instruction" (PSI) students study independently and sit a test for a unit whenever they feel ready. If they past the test they are given the objectives for the next unit. The main teaching comes when a student fails a test. Such approaches can be very cost-effective, being both economical and successful.

Tutors are unable to cope with the variety of students

Independence strategies

Independence strategies give responsibility to students to make use of a range of opportunities to suit their own varying needs. They can also place value on the progress students make in their learning rather than on the particular point they reach, so accepting differences in learning outcomes rather than seeing them as a problem to be avoided.

Variety of support mechanisms

Students can be offered optional self-check tests, remedial lectures, optional problem classes and surgeries, additional reading lists, optional self-help groups, access to additional video or computer-assisted learning material in the library and a whole host of other optional extras. Different students with different learning styles and preferences, as well as different needs, will take advantage of these extras to different extents. One-to-one tutorial support would be too expensive to provide for everyone, but few actually take advantage of surgery slots that must be booked in advance, so they can be provided quite cheaply. Similarly, CAL software and microcomputers for all students might be prohibitively expensive, but, available on open access in the library, would provide a valuable extra for those that chose to use them. The crucial element is student choice in taking advantage of opportunities.

Negotiated goals

Contract learning, in which learning goals are negotiated, allows students to set for themselves, and reach, targets that suit their level of experience and competence and match their aspirations. Students can negotiate for a contract which would get them a "C" grade if completed successfully, or an "A" grade if they are more ambitious. Different levels of support can be provided for students to enable them to achieve different objectives within the same course. Students always achieve different levels anyway and you can build this reality into your planning.

Problem 8:

Control strategies

Control strategies rely on extrinsic motivation, usually centred on the desire to pass teacher-set tests, or at least on the desire to avoid failing such tests.

Frequent testing

Modular courses, with their one-term or one-semester modules and extensive coursework assessment, often involve more regular assessment than conventional degree programmes in the UK. This can lead to very strategic students who know exactly how well they are doing. Students can spend the bulk of their learning time on assessed tasks, with deadlines providing the main motivation. In the Education case study describedin Section 10.8, computer-marked multiple choice question tests are used to keep students working regularly through the course.

High failure rates

In the UK imposed high failure rates are found largely on courses controlled by professions (Law, Banking, Accountancy) where pass rates may be as low as 50%. The high chance of failing leads to compliant and hard-working students regardless of the quality of the teaching or inherent interest of the material or the learning tasks. Outside of externally controlled professional courses, high failure rates are rare in the UK. They are very much more common in Europe and North America. In the UK it is still largely the case that a high failure rate is seen as a failure of the course, rather than a failure of the students. However, the power of high failure rates to control student behaviour is unlikely to go unexploited for long.

Tutors are unable to motivate students

Independence strategies

Independence strategies focus on intrinsic motivation: on students being interested because they are pursuing their own goals in their own ways, on the intrinsic engagement involved in problem-solving, and on the motivating energy of interaction in groups.

Learning contracts, problem-solving, group work

A number of the independence strategies mentioned above have the potential for high levels of student motivation, especially the use of learning contracts, problem-based learning and team work.

Using control and independence strategies together

In practice many courses, and most of the case studies in Section 10, use a variety of methods which involve a mixture of control and independence strategies. For example, the Education case study (Section 10.8) uses multiple choice tests as well as autonomous seminar groups with peer-assessment.

Strong elements of structure are often necessary in large classes to enable the operation of what might otherwise be unmanageable complexity and variety. And students like a clear framework within which to study. If things are too open-ended they will need more tutorial support, not less.

Clear structure to content can also allow students to make more choices and exercise some independence. For example, if a course is structured into a series of relatively self-contained units, each with its own objectives and sample test material, it can be possible for students to skip those units they find they can already handle and focus their attention on those units which will require more of their effort. It requires the discipline and structure of a control strategy to provide students with sufficient information to enable this kind of independence. Students in the Physics case study (Section 10.6) make choices about which of the support mechanisms to take advantage, of with the benefit of clear objectives and feedback from computer-marked multiple choice tests.

Highly structured courses can benefit greatly from independence strategies for part of their operation. For example, in a case study described in Jenkins and Gibbs (1992) the learning outcomes, and even the course syllabus listings, remained fixed by teachers. Students had to achieve much the same level of knowledge in specified areas as before if they were to succeed in the subsequent second year of the course, and still took teacher-set end-of-year exams. But the use of "study networks", involving learning teams, and "personal development workshops", involving reviews of learning needs and setting of personal learning goals, added a major new dimension to an otherwise teacher-centred course, and enabled the course to cope with increased class size at the same time.

In courses such as the Certificate in Management, where the syllabus and a list of competencies may be specified in considerable detail, the ways these are "covered" or achieved is sometimes negotiated between student and tutor through a series of college- or work-based learning contracts. There is considerable flexibility and independence which would have been hard to manage without the strong underlying structure. In fact, prior to the development of these lists of competencies and the use of learning contracts, students' work tended to be much narrower, more predictable in nature, and more focussed around series of lectures and examination demands.

On some courses, however, the strategies are mixed in ways which do not work. Students appear to be asked to be independent, while in reality they have little scope for manoeuvre and are rewarded for conformity. Students may be asked to work co-operatively in teams, but be set such predictable and pre-defined tasks that the group work is as controlled as if they were on their own following instructions. Students may be asked to be creative even where learning objectives are pre-specified and tests are tightly linked to these objectives. Students can be given conflicting messages about what the real task is and about what would count as acceptable performance on a course. The problem is usually that there is more control, and less scope for independence, than is claimed by teachers. Students' motivation and involvement soon suffers. Teachers complain that independence strategies do not work or that students are conservative in their study habits when the real problem is a confusion of strategies.

6 Alternative resource strategies

The patterns of expenditure on courses are often uniform: each course element is allocated the same notional budget of teaching and assessment time, accommodation or other resources as each other element. Where there are variations these may be due to historical precedent rather than strategic planning. To cope effectively with more students, resources have to be deployed strategically, using course designs which involve a wide range of costs per student. The following strategies are the most common.

6.1 Teach the first year cheaply - and the third year expensively

This is a very common strategy. Lower-level objectives may be easier to teach and much easier to assess. There may be less to discuss and negotiate. Scope for variations in what students do or learn may be constrained by the need to establish prerequisite knowledge for second-year courses, making economical control strategies suitable. Textbooks may provide adequate support without much further reading. Lectures may provide, at the minimum, a model of the way academics think and approach their discipline.

This strategy gives first-year students a rough deal compared with third-year students studying specialist options. Students' needs for social integration and the development of academic learning skills are not well served by large impersonal courses involving little discussion or individualised feedback. In addition, students may develop a passive, mechanical approach to learning which does not serve them well thereafter and which is difficult for tutors to change. In North America and Europe the cost of cheap first years is a high drop-out and failure rate.

6.2 Develop independence early

An alternative approach invests in developing students as learners early on. A case study in Jenkins and Gibbs (1992) describes a Sociology degree programme which spends twice as much per student in the first term as in the next two terms. There is a heavy investment in seminars and the development and assessment of library and other study skills. The students can then cope better with cheaper courses involving more independent learning without much support or feedback.

6.3 Vary your investment - and teach the mechanical bits cheaply

It is not just first-year courses that lend themselves to teaching and assessment in a very controlled and economical way. Some modules and course components involve well-defined objectives and skills which do not require the same level of discussion or personalised feedback as otherswhich are more controversial or open-ended in nature. Some topics are well served by standard textbooks, open-learning packages or computer-assisted learning material, while others require extensive background reading and individual tuition. Even within a module it may be possible to teach different parts in different ways. For example, the Physics case study (Section 10.6) uses a computer-assisted learning programme which enables one of the eight lab sessions to be handled outside the lab, achieving a worthwhile saving in staff and laboratory time.

6.4 Let go of some objectives - in order to hold on to others

It may not be realistic to attempt to hold on to all of the objectives of courses which used to be resourced at quite a different level. If it is no longer possible for every student to spend four hours in the lab each week for every science course they take, then tough decisions have to be made about what the real objectives of the lab work are, and which of these objectives it is least damaging to let go of. For example, collecting large quantities of data by using a piece of equipment in one way, while useful, may not be as valuable as brief experience of using the piece of equipment in a variety of different ways; to acknowledge this would have implications for the types of laboratory sessions used and the extent to which different objectives (such as processing large quantities of data) can be achieved outside the lab. As absolute limits are encountered in accommodation and staff time, tough decisions have to be made about what to drop first. Trying to hold on to a little bit of everything is likely to lead to a progressive degradation of quality.

6.5 Franchise introductory courses

Many higher-education institutions have higher unit costs and larger overheads than some colleges with substantial further-education components. It is becoming common for polytechnics to franchise nearby institutions to teach introductory and feeder courses because it is more economical that way. These courses may well not need the more expensive and sophisticated infrastructure, staff and laboratory or library facilities provided at present in the polytechnics.

6.6 Use students as tutors

Most American universities employ large numbers of postgraduate students as teaching assistants, and many institutions in the UK are developing a range of schemes to establish the similar use of postgraduates on a much wider scale. But it is not only postgraduates who can contribute. Third- or even second- year students can provide a valuable support service for first-year students where it would otherwise be impossible to provide any tuition. Students acting as teaching assistants can be given course credits, paid a modest fee, or simply, as at a number of polytechnics, undertake peer tuition as a valuable learning experience. Students generally welcome and greatly benefit from opportunities to act as tutors.

Students of a similar age to their tutees and who recently undertook and succeeded on the same course themselves can provide extremely relevant tuition to individuals or small groups. They can mark straightforward work such as mathematical problems or lab reports using marking schemes, and give useful feedback on more open-ended work such as essays. They can convene and support "self-help" groups and provide remedial tuition after short objective tests. They can demonstrate in labs (subject to Health and Safety regulations) and supervise fieldwork and visits. They can provide perfectly adequate first-line support in information technology training and computer use.

Early experience of the use of students as tutors makes it clear that they must be properly prepared and trained, and their role (and its limits) clearly defined. It is also necessary to provide some support after they have started because they can encounter difficulties and find the role stressful. There is tremendous scope for development in this area.

6.7 Use resource-based learning

The Open University has demonstrated just how little face-to-face tuition is necessary, in some circumstances, to support high-level learning. The Open Polytechnic has been launched partly to support widespread developments in the use of resource-based learning - mainly text-based learning packages. However, students do not come into full-time higher education expecting only to be told to go away again on their own with a learning package. The use of resource-based strategies must not imitate comprehensive distance-learning models but develop new approaches, which exploit what full-time residential learning in institutions has to offer as well as the benefits of well-designed learning resources. Comprehensive use of resource-based strategies, whether print, computer or multi-media based, requires a significant initial investment involving a diversion of resources away from funding teaching staff to teach, and such a strategy is more likely to come about through senior management decisions than grass-roots initiatives.

7 Course review questionnaire

This questionnaire is designed to help clarify some of the crucial features of your course, before you consider alternatives and start trying to map these out when re-designing your course.

Course title and level ....
Purposes or main aims of the course
Number of students: Present .... **Planned** ....
Main characteristics of the students as they affect teaching and learning methods
Main strengths of the current course, which you would not like to lose
What single thing that you do as a teacher on this course works best?
Main weaknesses of the course which need to be addressed
What are the main threats to quality posed by increasing numbers?
What would make teaching this course intolerable for you?

8 Teaching and study time

The proportion of students' total time learning on a course which is spent in class or with a tutor varies very widely. It is, of course, very different between subjects such as Chemistry and Engineering, which have considerable laboratory and practical elements, and English and Sociology, which require a great deal of independent reading. Part-time courses often involve a much higher proportion of class time even though the students are often mature and perfectly capable of studying independently. The proportion of teaching time also varies widely between the years of a course - it is not uncommon for undergraduate students to spend twice as much time on independent learning in the final year as in their first year. The kinds of variation which are common are displayed in the table below.

	Teaching hours	Study hours
1st year	25% - 50%	50% - 75%
2nd year	20% - 45%	55% - 80%
3rd year	15% - 35%	65% - 85%

It is interesting that there are also wide variations between institutions, within disciplines, with some courses involving far higher proportions of teaching time than others concerned with the same subject. It has been common for university courses to involve less teaching than polytechnic courses, and for polytechnic courses to involve less teaching than courses at colleges of higher education. It seems that it is possible to design and run very effective courses with half as much teaching at one institution as is assumed to be necessary at another institution.

The crucial issue seems to be not so much the quantity of teaching, but the effectiveness of the methods used to support high-quality independent learning. The highest-quality learning usually takes place in the final year when there is least teaching: often as little as 20% of students' total learning time. Instead of focussing entirely on what teachers do and on what class contact time is used for, perhaps we ought to be paying more attention to what students are doing when they are not in class, and designing our courses around this learning time. Class contact time should be perceived as the support necessary for effective independent learning.

This concern can be operationalised through the way courses are described in documentation. Normally a syllabus is listed and the teaching and assessment are specified as in the example below.

Teaching		Assessment	
Lectures:	20 hours	Coursework:	60%
Seminars:	10 hours	Exam:	40%
Tutorials:	2 hours		

This tells us nothing about how big the course is in terms of expected learning hours, what kinds of independent learning are expected or what kinds of tasks the coursework consists of. It gives no clues as to how effective this course is in generating productive independent learning hours. The notion of courses consisting of learning hours, rather than teaching hours, has become commonplace in the context of CATS (Credit Accumulation and Transfer Scheme) ratings and on modular courses, where the size of course units has to be calibrated in a way which is not dependent on the type of teaching patterns used, but rather on the learning demands they make.

In contrast, the course description below, drawn from a modular scheme where all modules are designed to be 120 learning hours in length, involves quite different information.

Title:
Geography and the Contemporary World

Teaching and learning methods:

This module is designed on the assumption that students will spend their 120 hours in the following ways:

4 hours in formal lectures

3 hours in workshops on library skills

6 hours in seminars to discuss project ideas

56 hours (5 days) in independent fieldwork investigation (details in the fieldwork guide)

10 hours in workshops to present and discuss the outcomes of the fieldwork investigations

2 hours in tutorials

18 hours preparing a project notebook for assessment (6 hours reading, 12 hours writing)

21 hours preparing reports: 6 hours on a resource paper and 15 hours per student preparing a group project report (6 hours reading, 6 hours writing and 3 hours in group meetings).

Assessment

100% coursework:
- 15% for the project notebook
- 60% for the final project report
- 25% for the group workshop presentations

Everything students are required to do has to be accounted for. If they need to revise for an exam then the hours for this revision have to be included in the course specification and some other element of the course has to be reduced or scrapped. The lecturer who designed this course had to be aware that he had only 120 hours of student time to play with and had to think carefully about how to best use this time. If he had included too much class contact time there would not have been enough time left for the individual and group independent work.

Notice how class contact hours are used here to develop library skills, develop project ideas and discuss the outcomes of independent work, rather than just to present information. The teaching has been designed around the desired independent study, not the other way round. The teaching here represents only 21% of the total learning time for a course which operates at the start of the second year of a degree programme.

Of course students do not actually spend their time as specified in the course description. Some work more or less hard, some skip the lectures or read less. But this design exercise forces the lecturer to think about how s/he would like the students to work and guides the students as to what is expected. Some elements of the course may take longer than planned. This is an issue for evaluation. It is common on science courses, for example, for students to read very little (despite the impressive reading lists) because the lecturers have misjudged how long students take to write up lab reports and there is simply no time left for reading.

In re-designing courses to cope with more students it is vital to conceptualise the task as one of generating effective independent learning hours and thinking of the teaching input necessary to achieve this, rather than one of thinking how you are going to find the staff to fill all those class contact hours your course outline specifies.

To start this re-conceptualisation, specify in the framework below how your current course is broken down in terms of all the learning hours students spend on it. Calculate the total number of hours involved and the proportion of these hours which involve teaching.

Teaching and study time analysis

Hours inside class/ in contact with tutors		**Hours outside class/ independent study**	
Activity	Hours	Activity	Hours
....	....	....	....
....	....	....	....
....	....	....	....
....	....	....	....
....	....	....	....
....	....	....	....
....	....	....	....
....	....	....	....
....	....	....	....
....	....	....	....
....	....	....	....
....	....	....	....
....	....	....	....
....	....	....	....
....	....	....	....
Total teaching hours	....	Total independent study hours	....
Total hours for the course		....	
Teaching hours as a % of total		.........%	

9 Teaching and learning methods for more students

The ideas and methods outlined in brief here are described in more detail in the other booklets in this series: *Lecturing to More Students, Discussion with More Students, Assessing More Students* and *Independent Learning with More Students.* Those summarised here are the most significant in terms of course re-design and are offered as a resource for course re-design.

9.1 Lecturing to more students

Active learning in large lectures

Although it is easier to lecture effectively to smaller groups, it is possible to engage students actively even in very large classes. A variety of breaks and tasks can involve reflection, discussion and application of concepts during large lectures. As well as offering ways of overcoming problems to do with lapses of attention, inaccurate note-taking and forgetting, these activities can model the forms of analysis required during independent learning and can provide some of the social integration which is often lacking with more students.

As active learning during large lectures takes up some of the time which would otherwise have been devoted to straight presentation, it is usually necessary to plan for giving students access to additional material. This may involve learning packages, use of textbooks, or the development of improved library and reading skills.

Abandoning or cutting down on lectures

Because lectures, and especially large lectures, achieve only a limited range of educational goals, some courses choose to cut down on or completely abandon lectures (as in the Management, English and Mathematics case studies in Section 10). This clearly requires careful attention to the ways in which students get access to the course material; such access can be through printed lecture notes, textbooks, copyright-cleared readings, learning packages which guide them to a wide range of sources in the library and elsewhere, or even computers. The Physics case study (Section 10.6) involves a textbook, a workbook and computer-assisted learning material.

9.2 Discussion with more students

Larger seminar groups

On many courses the bulk of the teaching costs are not associated with lectures, but with small-group discussions. As group size gets bigger these work less well and stop serving their intended purpose of actively involving all students in discussion. A wide range of techniques is available for structuring discussion groups so that students become actively involved even though the group may be as large as 30. This inevitably means less direct discussion with the tutor, but more discussion with other students, in pairs or sub-groups in various ways. These "workshop" type sessions can be very effective and popular with students. They clearly achieve slightly different goals from very small tutor-led unstructured sessions, but they do offer a viable and cost-effective alternative.

Parallel and independent groups

If students can discuss productively in sub-groups within a large workshop-type session, without the immediate presence of the tutor, then they can also discuss effectively within smaller tutor-less seminar groups. Increasingly courses are setting up autonomous seminar groups which run in parallel, with a tutor (or team of tutors if there are very large numbers of parallel groups) touring between groups to check that everything is OK. These independent groups often need clear guidelines as to how to operate and may need brief training. Some courses insist on a particular format of meeting, even involving an agenda, chair, secretary and minutes, which are handed in for checking or assessment. It may help to use peer-assessment of seminar presentations to add a little bite to the sessions. Students can also be expected to meet in their seminar groups before and after a session with the tutor, to prepare and to de-brief, so as to make maximum use of the precious time spent with the tutor.

9.3 Independent learning

Learning packages

Course guides, which explain the course aims, teaching sessions, assessment and reading resources, are almost obligatory for very large courses. Learning packages often grow from such course guides rather than being designed from scratch. They may contain copyright-cleared reading material, specially written explanations, detailed guidance to set reading in textbooks, lecture notes or summaries of lectures, notes on seminars, exercises and detailed briefings for assignments and projects. Usually they do not look like Open University material, in that the bulk of the course content is elsewhere (in lectures or the library, for example), but they support the independent study which students need to undertake. If there were only lectures and no learning packages, students would flounder or be forever knocking on their tutor's door asking for help.

Learning teams

It is becoming increasingly common to set up "self-help" groups on a formal basis, not just for the organised and enthusiastic but for everybody. They may submit draft assignments to each other for feedback or even for peer-assessment. They may meet to prepare before laboratory sessions or seminars. They may share reading material and brief each other on what they have read, or share computer terminals and discuss what they are doing. Learning teams may be the same as seminar groups within a particular course or may operate independently and support their members in whatever studies they undertake. Learning teams can have a dramatic effect on the motivation and social integration of students in addition to what they learn from each other. They require planning, advice and support on a continuing basis. You cannot expect learning teams to form and continue for long without taking them seriously and integrating their activities into the operation of courses.

Project teams

Instead of students working on assignments in competitive isolation, they can be required to co-operate in teams. Almost any assignment can be turned into a team assignment. This benefits the students as well as cutting down on supervision and marking time. Project teams can co-operate on laboratory work, essays, reports, seminar presentations and fieldwork, as well as on major projects. The products of team work are almost always of higher quality than the products of isolated individuals.

Co-operation in teams is not easy and students can be very bad at it. It is important to provide support, guidance, even training, and to use an assessment method which does not allow individuals to ride on the efforts of others but which rewards the relative contributions of individuals to the products of the team work.

Independent learning skills

If class contact time and the opportunity to gain one-to-one help from tutors is to be reduced, students will need to become more skilful and resourceful in studying independently. This does not come about all on its own. You will need to develop students' library search skills so that they can cope when the recommended text is unavailable. You will need to develop co-operative group skills so that students can support each other outside class or in autonomous seminar groups. You will need to develop writing skills because there will be little opportunity for personal guidance. You will need to develop time- and task-management skills because more of their time will be spent on independent learning.

Investment in developing independent learning skills can pay off handsomely by making possible types of course design which students can cope with and which foster efficient learning. Ignoring the need for these skills can wreck a course.

9.4 Assessment

Mechanising assessment

Assessment can be very expensive on large courses - sometimes costing more than the teaching. Not all of this investment of staff time is productive. Some aspects of assessment can be mechanised very effectively, leaving tutors to devote their time to those aspects which cannot be mechanised. The two main forms of mechanisation are the use of multiple choice question tests, preferably computer-marked, and the use of assignment attachment forms.

MCQ tests have been used extensively for many years in Medicine and other areas and are almost universal in North America. There is plenty of scope for extending their use to assess certain educational objectives efficiently without compromising the overall objectives of a course. The key issue here is diversity: assess lower-level objectives cheaply using one set of methods so that expensive tutor time can be used to assess higher-level objectives. MCQ tests can also be used to provide students with feedback on their progress (as in the Physics case study in Section 10.6) and as parts of tests - for example, to replace the short-answer section at the beginning of most science and technology exam papers. Contrary to popular conceptions, MCQs, properly constructed, can be used to test high-level conceptual skills, analysis and application of concepts as well as mastery of factual information. Writing such MCQs is, however, a skilful business. Extensive sets of ready-made MCQs are often available to support American textbooks and you may not need to design your own.

Assignment attachment forms structure the feedback tutors give on written work: labs, essays and reports. They can give a comprehensive overview of a piece of work in relation to a clearly defined set of criteria and can save marking time as well. One of their advantages is that their clarity helps to orientate students towards your desired goals, so that fewer students will submit work which is way off-beam and which therefore takes a long time to respond to.

Self- and peer-assessment

Self- and peer-assessment can be used in three main ways: to increase the quality of feedback to students on their work, to orientate students more clearly towards the kinds of performance you require of them, and to save marking time. The last of these is the hardest to achieve. In scientific and technical areas marking sheets can be used to guide self- and peer-marking (as explained in a case study in Booklet 4: *Assessing More Students*). However, it is difficult to save the tutor's time in "softer" subjects because checking students' marking can take nearly as long as marking the work yourself.

Significant gains can be achieved, however, in certain areas. For example, given clear guidelines and practice at calibrating their judgements, students can do a decent job of assessing their peers' seminar presentations, and this may require little supervision and monitoring (as in the Education case study in Section 10.8).

The main benefits, however, are likely to be from self-assessment, helping students to supervise themselves and improve their own work before it is submitted, and peer-assessment as a tutorial process, in which students give each other guidance on problems (as in the Mathematics case study in Section 10.7) or feedback on first drafts before work is submitted. As it becomes harder for tutors to provide detailed guidance to each individual student, so self- and peer-assessment can substitute for this guidance to some extent. Self- and peer-assessment need not contribute to marks to be a valuable process; and the desired number of written assignments can be maintained by using peer-assessment as a feedback process and not marking the work.

Assessing groups instead of individuals

There is enormous scope for saving marking time by assessing group rather than individual work for some of the time. The products of group work may be longer than the products of individual work, but marking the product of a group of six may take 50% longer rather than six times as long. These products are also likely to have been more carefully checked in advance and to be of a higher quality than individual work, which can also save marking time. A variety of strategies can be used to allocate marks to individuals within groups in a fair way which acknowledges the different contributions of individuals, and this need not take much of the tutor's time to do: peer-assessment can be appropriate here.

10 Case studies in course re-design

Introduction

These case studies are intended to illustrate the ways in which courses can be re-designed to accommodate more students, and also to demonstrate the costing of courses in terms of staff hours. Each case study includes a description of the original course alongside a re-designed alternative, together with a costing in a standard format.

These cases are all based on real courses: six in polytechnics and two in universities. They have been simplified to some extent for ease of presentation, and also disguised to some extent for the sake of anonymity. For the first four the alternative course designs are speculative. These are possibilities which have been discussed with the course teams concerned. The last four involve descriptions of re-designs which have been implemented and the accounts include evidence from what actually happened, though again details have been simplified and disguised.

All these case studies produce dramatic savings in staff costs - over 60% savings in some cases - as well as potential or actual benefits in quality and student performance. Dramatic savings of these kinds may not always be necessary, but the case studies illustrate what is possible.

The costings demonstrate where costs are generated. For example, the assessment system may cost more than the teaching, as with the Physics course (case study 6) where the assessment cost twice as much as the teaching. This enables you to focus attention on the most important areas for savings. The inclusion of a measure of the cost per student for teaching, assessment and in total allows you to recognise overall savings and to recognise the relative costs of different courses.

10.1 Biology

This is a first-year undergraduate course for 320 students, with laboratory work to develop data-collection skills and practical workshops to develop data-handling skills. The bulk of the teaching time is generated by the small-group workshops and the assessment time is generated by individual lab and workshop reports. The alternative uses only 46% of the staff hours yet increases the amount of assessment, feedback on assessment and discussion.

The alternative course design has the following main features:

- Lectures are retained.

- Students are formed into learning teams. They undertake their laboratory and practical work in these teams and submit team assignments.

- A course guide supports students by providing information about the lectures, labs and workshops, guidance on team work and on the poster and report assignments, MCQs for self-testing and a reading list.

- Instead of the individual data-collection report, each of 80 teams of four produces two posters, displayed in the corridor outside the labs. A lecturer spends ten minutes assessing and commenting on each of the 160 posters instead of 15 minutes assessing each of the 320 lab reports. Despite each student being involved in two pieces of work instead of one, the marking takes one third of the time. All the students can see one another's posters and the comments on them, and can learn from this.

- The workshops in groups of eight are replaced by workshops with eight teams of four. As these teams work together throughout the course they will be able to handle many of their own problems and one tutor will be able to handle eight teams nearly as well as eight individuals. These workshop sessions are more demanding but very much less repetitive than before.

- The individual data-handling reports are replaced by team reports. Students simply gain the team mark, without moderation.

- Individual marks come from the four MCQ tests, each related to one of the four laboratory sessions. These are computer-marked and the only staff time involved is in their administration and in record-keeping.

Investment in change involves writing the course guide and the MCQs and learning to run larger workshop sessions and to mark posters. As the savings each year amount to416 staff hours, this investment should not be hard to justify.

Current course	Staff time (hours)		Proposed alternative
Teaching			
	—	4	Team-building exercise
20 Lectures	20	20	20 interactive lectures supported by learning package
4 x 4.5-hour labs undertaken individually, 5 staff for each of 5 lab splits with 64 students	450	270	4 x 4.5-hour labs undertaken in teams of four 3 staff for each of 5 lab splits with 16 teams
8 x 1-hour workshops 40 classes of 8	320	80	8 x 1-hour workshops teams of 4 in 10 classes of 32
Total teaching hours	790	374	
Total teaching hours/student	2.47	1.17	
47% of current teaching costs			

Current Course	**Staff Time (hours)**		**Proposed Alternative**
Assessment			
2 individual reports:			2 team posters, one team report + MCQ tests:
data collection (320 at 15 mins)	80	27	2 team posters (160 at 10 mins)
data handling (320 at 15 mins)	80	27	Team report (80 at 20 mins)
		16	4 MCQ tests (at 4 hours per test)
Total assessment hours	160	70	
Total assessment hours/student	0.50	0.22	
44% of current assessment costs			
Total staffing hours	950	444	
Total staffing hours/student	2.96	1.38	
46% of current total staffing costs			

10.2 Sociology

This is a first-year introductory course within a modular programme. The 26-week three-term course for 200 students is taught by means of two lectures and a seminar per week and is assessed by three essays, a seminar presentation and two three-hour exams. Lectures are divided into two groups of 100 and seminars into 20 groups of ten. The bulk of the teaching hours is generated by the seminars, and the bulk of the assessment hours is generated by essay-marking. The course has rapidly increased in size from 80 only three years before without any changes in course design. Considerable increases in student numbers are expected, up to as many as 400. Further scaling up of the volume of teaching and assessment hours is simply impossible within the existing staffing limits in the department.

The costings assume 400 students. The alternative course involves a range of changes:

- It reduces the number of lectures to one a week and gives them once, to the whole group of 400. This lecture is an overview of the week's work. Detailed information is obtained from a textbook, guided by a specially written workbook, and from wider reading supported by additional investment in library stock.

- It revolves around the operation of autonomous seminar groups of ten. Tutor-led seminars are limited to the start and end of each term - to set up the autonomous seminar groups and to review the term. The remainder of the seminars are run by students themselves and are peer-assessed. While 20 seminar groups run in parallel (twice a week, to accommodate the 40 seminar groups) four tutors each "tour" five seminar groups to check they are OK.

- Eight interactive "workshops" are introduced (three in each of terms 1 and 2, two in term 3) in ten groups of 40, in which seminar groups mix in cross-over sub-groups of four to undertake data analysis and interpretation activities under the direction of a tutor.

- Coursework assessment is still by three essays, but now students must obtain peer feedback and complete a self-assessment sheet before submitting each essay. The first essay the tutor marks in full as before. The second relies more on students' own feedback and the third relies heavily on peer- and self-assessment, leading to a 70% saving on the essays and 42% saving overall by reducing the need for detailed feedback. Seminar presentations (four by each pair of seminar presenters in each group) are peer- assessed and this peer-assessment is merely monitored for standards by the "touring" tutors. One of the two exams is replaced by a MCQ test to check that students have acquired a broad knowledge.

This alternative increases student independence and active involvement, provides plenty of peer support, increases opportunities for discussion, increases the amount of assessment and feedback, provides structured and accessible reading material, and yet costs only 41% as much in terms of total staffing hours. This represents a saving of 1165 hours - the equivalent of two full-time academic staff who could be developing and improving the course instead of being involved in massively repetitive teaching and marking.

It gives students less opportunity to be with their tutors in small groups and less tutor feedback on essays, and would require an organised personal tutor system or regular "surgery" hours for students with problems.

It requires investment in writing the workbook, rewriting the lectures, writing the MCQ tests (and possibly in acquiring the optical mark reader and microcomputer to mark them) and funding for the library. It also requires staff development to learn how to support parallel seminar groups, run workshops, give lectures to groups of 400 and use self- and peer-assessment as part of the marking process.

Current course (calculated for 400 students)	**Staff time (hours)**		**Proposed alternative**
Teaching			
Lectures (26 weeks x 2 x 4 groups of 100)	208	26	Lectures (26 weeks x 1 group of 400)
Seminars (26 weeks x 40 groups of 10)	1040	240	Tutor-led seminars (6 weeks x 40 groups of 10)

Current course (calculated for 400 students)	Staff time (hours)		Proposed alternative
		160	Student-led seminars (20 weeks x 4 tutors each supporting 5 groups of 10, twice a week)
		80	Workshops (8 weeks x 10 groups of 40)
Total teaching hours	1248	506	
Total teaching hours/student	3.12	1.27	
41% of current teaching costs			
Assessment			
3 essays (3 x 400 at 20 mins)	400	107	3 essays: tutor-, peer- and self-assessed
1 individual seminar assessment (400 at 10 mins)	67	67	4 x peer-assessment of seminars given by pairs (4 x 200 x 5 mins checking)
2 x 3-hour exams (2 x 400 at 20 mins)	267	133	1 x 3-hour exam (1 x 400 at 20 mins)
		4	MCQ test (at 4 hours)
Total assessment hours	734	311	
Total assessment hours/student	1.84	0.78	
42% of current assessment costs			
Total staffing hours	1982	817	
Total staffing hours/student	4.96	2.04	
41% of current total staffing costs			

10.3 Psychology

This first-year course has already suffered from massive increases in student numbers (from 60 to 300) without commensurate increases in staffing, and the quality of student experience has declined. It involves two two-hour lectures each week for 24 weeks in which students are split into four groups of 75, and a three-hour practical class each week with students in groups of 25. The lecture theatre cannot take more than 75 and the lab cannot take more than 25 within Health and Safety regulations. Staff therefore have to deliver each of the two two-hour lectures four times a week and supervise the same lab 12 times a week, every week: 16 hours of lectures and 36 hours of labs a week! There is no discussion outside the practicals - no seminars and no tutorials. Students submit only one essay for assessment in the whole year, and only one practical report from the 24 labs they do. There are two three-hour exams to compensate for the lack of coursework. The course has been stripped bare. The library is completely inadequate with a limited range of texts, few journals, limited multiple copies of standard texts and not enough seating space. A further substantial increase in student numbers is expected for each of the next three years at least.

This is an introductory course: only 75 students will go on to study Psychology further and only they will need the laboratory experience for British Psychological Society membership. The real goal for all other students is to provide a basic grounding in Psychology for students studying other subjects. The proposed alternative is therefore to teach two versions of the course: one general course providing a better grounding in Psychology for non-Psychology students and additional elements for Psychology students to give more lab experience. The main constraints are accommodation (lack of large lecture theatres and laboratories) and the library.

The proposed alternative has the following features:

- A single two-hour lecture is given to each of four groups of 75 students per week.

- A standard large American textbook is adopted, complete with study guide and both self-test MCQs and MCQ tests for assessment. The whole course is designed around this text. Key references are purchased in bulk for short loan in the library. Copyright clearance is gained for the photocopying of important articles and chapters, and the material is sold to students at a price to cover the reprographics.

- Learning teams of five are set up to provide opportunities for discussion, and peer support. These teams undertake two essays and all their practicals together.

- Students sit six MCQ tests which are computer-marked. They sit them individually but get the average score for their team. This has the effect of making everyone tutor everyone else so that they are not let down by their colleagues.

- Practicals are retained but fewer experiments are undertaken (eight instead of 24). Students work in their labs in teams, allowing more data to be collected faster (two hours instead of three) with less equipment and supervision.

- 16 further lab sessions are provided for the 75 students who need the experience to meet BPS requirements, and who will pursue Psychology as a subject in the second year.

- Teams discuss their practical work in workshops (in the groups of 25 formed for their practical classes). At these workshops they present posters of their practical work for discussion. Four of these are written up as reports by each team for assessment.

- As students work from the set text, work so much co-operatively and discuss more, they need far fewer lectures and these can be made interactive, involving the learning teams in discussion and activities during the lectures.

- The assessment is so much more comprehensive that only one final exam is required.

The alternative introduces extensive opportunities for discussion, quadruples practical write-ups, introduces frequent MCQ testing, doubles the essay-writing, partly solves the library problem and yet saves 885 staff hours, or 58% of staff resources. It reduces lab experience for non-Psychology students but focusses on the main objectives much more puposefully, and provides the necessary lab experience for those who need it.

Current course (calculated for 400 students)	Staff time (hours)		Proposed alternative
Teaching			
Lectures (24 weeks x 2 x 2 hours, x 4 groups of 75)	384	96	Interactive lectures (24 weeks x 2 hours, x 4 groups of 75)
Practicals (24 x 3 hours x 12 groups of 25)	864	192	Practicals (8 x 2 hours x 12 groups of 25)
		96	Workshops (8 x 1 hour x 12 groups of 25)
		96	Practicals for Psychology students (16 x 2 hours x 3 groups of 25)
Total teaching hours	1248	480	
Total teaching hours/student	4.16	1.6	
38% of the teaching costs			
Assessment			
1 essay (300 at 15 mins)	75	30	2 essays (2 x 60 teams of 5 at 15 mins)
		18	6 x MCQ tests (at 3 hours per test)
1 practical report (300 at 15 mins)	75	60	4 practical reports (4 x 60 teams of 5 at 15 mins)
2 x 3-hour exams (2 x 300 at 15 mins)	150	75	1 x 3-hour exam (1 x 300 at 15 mins)
Total assessment hours	300	183	
Total assessment hours/student	1.00	0.61	
61% of assessment costs			
Total staffing hours	1548	663	
Total staffing hours/student	5.16	2.21	
42% of total staff costs			

10.4 English

This case study addresses the issue of maintaining quality with more students rather than focussing on the resource issues. It involves a second-year course in Victorian Literature on an English degree programme. The course was a "survey" course taught by a team of lecturers each with their own favourite authors, interests and specialisms. Any number of possible Victorian Literature courses could have been taught which were logically coherent and reasonably comprehensive. The course consisted of a lecture and a seminar each week. At the seminars one student was supposed to have read around a topic and the others were supposed to have read the key text for the week. In practice students did not do enough reading and the seminars were often of poor quality and usually ended up being led by the tutor. Assessment was by three essays (one per term) and a three-hour exam. Student motivation was not high and independence, in studying and in thought, was not as evident as it should have been. The diagnosis was that the programme was not very coherent, lectures led to passivity and students had too little opportunity to choose their own topics and texts, and that the seminars did not work at all well. Much of this was due to increased class size and the staff simply not knowing the students well any more.

Numbers were increasing rapidly from an initial level of around 50 to 144 when this re-design was undertaken, and this was making the maintenance of the pattern of teaching and learning methods unsustainable. There was no desire to reduce teaching hours drastically and it was felt important to retain both the volume of seminars and the volume of writing and feedback if quality was to be maintained.

The re-designed course has the following key features:

- The seminars are made central to the whole course and a session put aside at the start of the year to develop seminar presentation skills and group skills, and to explain the way in which seminar presentations and seminar write-ups will be assessed.

- In each seminar group of eight, pairs of students take turns to give joint presentations. Of five presentations for each pair in the year, the first is for practice and the remaining four are to be assessed by the tutor at the end of the seminar, using clearly stated criteria. This is designed to make students take the seminars seriously.

- Lectures abandoned. This is not to save time but because they led to a passive approach and constrained the topics students studied.

- The seminar programme is designed by each seminar group so that the students are highly motivated to pursue their own interests. Students are required to meet together in their seminar groups before each seminar to ensure proper preparation and maximum use of the tutor at the seminar.

- A day-long session is held at the end of the students' first year, at which these seminar programmes are developed. During this day an overview lecture on Victorian Literature is presented, students are taken on a library tour to show the resources available and each of the tutors presents an exhibition "selling their wares" and interesting students in their specialist topics. Students then have the rest of the day, with the support of the tutors, to devise their own programme for the year, specifying a key text for the whole group to read for each week. This programme is modified in negotiation with the course leader to ensure a reasonably coherent structure and adequate coverage of key themes.

- Because students are assessed on four seminar presentations and one seminar write-up (of their own choice), there is a need for only two essays and two questions on the exam (compared with three essays and three questions in the original course).

Overall, the re-design saves only 22% of staff costs (176 hours) but the seminars are much more likely to work well. Students will be more highly motivated, both through the assessment and through their own choice of seminar topics and texts, and will have more discussion and social contact through their seminar group. The course becomes more student-centred and involves more discussion and feedback on work, as well as being cheaper to run.

The lectures could be re-introduced on an optional basis to support the seminar programme, if this was felt necessary, while adding only a modest amount to the teaching costs.

Current course (calculated for 144 students)	**Staff time (hours)**		**Proposed alternative**
Teaching			
Lectures	22	20	Preparation for "launch" day
Seminars (22 weeks x 24 groups of 6)	528	6	Setting up seminar groups
		396	Seminars (22 weeks x 18 groups of 8)
Total teaching hours	550	422	
Total teaching hours/student	3.81	2.93	
	77% of current teaching costs		

Current course (calculated for 144 students)	Staff time (hours)		Proposed alternative
Assessment			
3 essays (144 x 3 = 432 at 20 mins)	144	96	2 essays (144 x 2 = 288 at 20 mins)
		—	Seminar presentations (4 x 70 pairs - during seminars)
		24	Seminar write-up (72 x 2 write ups at 10 mins)
Exams (3 questions x 144 at 10 mins)	72	48	Exam (2 questions x 144 at 10 mins)
Total assessment hours	216	168	
Total assessment hours/student	1.50	1.16	
	78% of current assessment costs		
Total staffing hours	766	590	
Total staffing hours/student	5.32	4.10	
	78% of current total staffing costs		

10.5 Management

This case study is based on a one-year professional updating course for the hotel and catering industry. Its syllabus was controlled by and its examinations set and marked by an external professional body. The syllabus is excessively large and the national pass rate for the exam at the time the re-design was carried out was about 50%. The particular course studied here was averaging below 50% despite attempts to improve the lectures and the students' study skills.

The Management element of the course was taught exclusively by lectures to a group of 25 - 30. To get through the syllabus six lectures were given each week. Other parts of the course were similarly heavily taught and students had little time to read or study independently. They also had little opportunity to bring their own experience of the industry to bear on the management concepts they were being taught.

Student numbers were due to increase, making it even less likely that students would participate in the lectures.

The alternative involved a radical change. The lectures were abandoned as a means of conveying information and were replaced by two textbooks and a comprehensive set of learning packages: one for each week of the course. Each learning package contained:

- Learning objectives: an unambiguous statement of what the students should be able to do at the end of the week.

- Key-word notes. These resembled what the students might have written down if both they and the lecturer had been on good form in the lectures. They also contained detailed references for follow-up reading, referring to specific pages in the textbooks and other material.

- A bibliography for wider reading.

- Self-assessment short-answer questions which allowed students to test themselves in relation to the objectives.

- Past exam question on the topics covered that week, so that students could see the kinds of larger-scale question they would eventually have to be able to answer.

- A case study, set in the context of the hotel and catering industry, illustrating that week's management concepts.

The week's work for a student, in the alternative course, consisted of attending a session at the start of the week in which the lecturer outlined the topic for the week, the concepts to be examined, and the case study which students would work on. This lecture was not used for conveying basic information, which was handled by the learning packages and textbooks.

The students then worked independently, going through the learning package, referring to the textbooks, looking things up in the further reading and analysing the case study.

At the end of the week there was a two-hour session in which students were formed into syndicate groups and discussed the case study. They were given specific questions about the study to consider. The tutor toured the groups offering help, and gave an overview of the case study in a plenary session towards the end of the two hours.

The alternative course design costed here was implemented for several years and led to a dramatic improvement in pass rates to an average of about 80%. The costings of neither the original design nor the alternative are sensitive to student numbers as all students attend all sessions and there is no coursework or internally marked final examination.

Original course (calculated for 40 students)	**Staff time (hours)**		**Alternative course**
Teaching			
Lectures (26 weeks x 6)	156	26	Lectures (26 weeks x 1)
		52	Workshops (26 weeks x 2 hours)
Total teaching hours	156	78	
Total teaching hours/student	3.9	1.95	
	50% of former teaching costs		

Despite dramatically improving the chances that students would pass the exam, and despite halvingthe amount of time spent in class, the course evaluation showed that students did not particularly like the format of the course. They believed the lecturer should have been giving them lectures! However, they were clearly wrong. Had they been given lectures more than half of them (on previous experience) would have failed the course. This raises the important point that students do not always know what is good for them. The alternative course required more independent work and less passive sitting in lectures. Students did not like this hard work but it did them a great deal of good. Evaluation data should be interpreted with great care!

The work involved in writing the learning packages was considerable and could not have been achieved without special support. This came in the form of a grant used to buy in 60 hours of part-time teaching help to release the lecturer concerned. This investment was more than re-couped in the first year of operation of the new course. Once the packages had been written it was possible to increase student numbers with no additional costs and with significantly better results than before.

The lecturer involved reported that the greatest benefit, from his point of view, was that the new course was far less stressful to deliver.

10.6 Physics

This case study illustrates a number of important features of the process of change to cope with more students. Over a period of three years, and six operations of the course, a succession of incremental changes and adjustments were made. The lecturer concerned was learning how to manage a large course alone, with new methods and new types of student, by experimentation and careful evaluation. By the end more than three times as many students were being accommodated at half the staff costs per student and with better exam results. This was achieved through a highly structured approach involving clear objectives and the targetting of support on those who needed it.

The original course was taken by 40 students as their first Physics module on a modular Physics degree programme. The content was typical of such courses, designed to establish a sound understanding of basic concepts encountered at A-level before moving on to more advanced material in subsequent modules. It was also typical in process, consisting of a series of three lectures each week and weekly laboratory sessions supported by smaller group discussions. Assessment was by two problem sheets, eight lab reports and an examination.

Not only did student numbers grow to 100 within two years (and to 150 since) but the students taking the course changed. Engineering Foundation students and those on "Women into Engineering" schemes started taking the course. Almost all the increase in numbers came from students who were not going on to study more Physics and those who had little Physics background.

The changes involved the development of a workbook, the location and purchase of computer-assisted learning software, the introduction of computer-marked tests and the use of surgeries for individual students. These elements were introduced incrementally and a variety of changes were made in the details of operation in response to problems and to student feedback. The alternative described here is based on that operating in 1990, two years after the changes began. The main features of the alternative were:

- Students attended at least two lectures.

- After the lecture students used a workbook which specified objectives clearly and provided self-check multiple choice questions.

- Students used a set text: an American textbook which made appropriate assumptions about the mathematical background abilities of the students.

- Most laboratory sessions were retained, but all except three were written up only in note form. Three were written up in full for assessment. One lab was replaced by a computer-assisted learning programme: each student was provided with a copy of the software and had to learn to use a PC to work through it. Further back-up video and computer simulation material was provided in the library.

- A multiple choice question test was set towards the end of each week, in a lecture theatre. The results were available to the students and the lecturer 12 hours later, and a follow-up lecture and small-group problem sessions were provided on those topics the students were poor at. The test results were purely for feedback and guidance and formed no part of the formal assessment.

- Students made their own decisions whether, after having undertaken the lab session and independent work with the workbook and textbook, they needed to take the MCQ test. When they got the results back they made up their own minds whether to attend the remedial lecture and problem class. They then decided for themselves whether they needed to take advantage of the surgeries.

- Two hours of surgery time were offered, in ten-minute slots. Students could sign up for these slots to sort out specific problems and queries.

The problem classes and surgery slots could be resourced only if a minority of students used them. But armed with clear objectives, test results and explanations in the remedial lecture, most students realised that they did not need further help. Perhaps 60% attended the remedial lecture, 40% the problem classes and 10% the surgeries. In this way expensive small-group and individual help was targetted on those who needed it and not wasted on those that did not.

Course in 1988 (calculated for 40 students)	Staff time (hours)		Course in 1990 (calculated for 100 students)
Teaching			
Lectures (8 weeks x 3 hours)	24	24	Lectures (8 weeks x 3 hours)
Labs (8 weeks x 3 hours x 2 groups of 20)	48	84	Labs (7 weeks x 3 hours x 4 groups of 25)
Problem classes/seminars (8 weeks x 1 hour x 3 groups of 13)	24	24	Optional problem classes (8 weeks x 1 hour x 3 groups of 8-15)
		16	Surgery time (8 weeks x 12 x 10 mins)
Total teaching hours	96	148	
Total teaching hours/student	2.4	1.48	
62% of former teaching costs/student			
Assessment			
Problem sheets (2 x 40 at 20 mins)	27	--	CAL exercise
Lab reports (8 x 40 at 30 mins)	160	150	Lab reports (3 x 100 at 30 mins)
		50	Lab notes (100 at 30 mins)
Exam (40 at 30 mins)	20	50	Exam (100 at 30 mins)
Total assessment hours	207	250	
Total assessment hours/student	5.18	2.50	
48% of former assessment costs/student			
Total staffing hours	303	398	
Total staffing hours/student	7.58	3.98	
53% of former total staffing costs/student			

10.7 Mathematics

This case study deals with one of a whole range of Mathematics modules at the institution concerned which have progressively reduced dependence on lectures through providing full lecture notes. Initially the modules involved up to four lectures a week supported by problem classes. Eventually some modules were taught only through problem classes.

The module described here started with four lectures a week and problem classes in groups of about 18. As numbers increased the lectures became almost completely ineffective. The lecturer copied his own notes on to the board, virtually reading out what he was writing, and students wrote it all down verbatim, or at least as accurately as they could manage at the speed the lecture went. When classes had been smaller than 30 there were enough questions to make this process reasonably effective, but as class size increased the process broke down. Because the class was large, and because of the demands of writing down unfamiliar mathematics at such speed, few questions were asked. Lectures became an expensive and error-strewn reprographic technique which took up a great deal of lecturer's and students' time. Because the lectures had become so passive, students arrived at problem classes not having understood the mathematics. The problem classes quickly turned into lectures to smaller groups as the same basic queries and difficulties cropped up again and again. Attendance at both lectures and problem classes was high because there was no other way of finding out what the course consisted of. Exam results were disappointing, with much evidence of students not understanding the mathematics.

The alternative design retained one lecture a week, to give an introduction to the week's material, and to talk students through the notes and problems. The lectures were written out in full, together with a commentary and "asides" and handed out to students in a series of lecture-note packages at the start of the module. An additional package contained a selection of the kinds of problems which would be tackled in the weekly problem classes. A textbook was recommended for further explanation of the mathematics (using the same notation and a similar approach). Students worked independently from the lecture notes and problem package and then attended a problem class. In the problem classes they were arranged in groups of four and peer-assessed one another's attempts at problems, using marking sheets. Most points were therefore handled by students themselves as they handed marked problems back to each other. The tutor then toured the groups picking up on what still needed explaining. Only if the same issues were raised by a succession of groups did he give an impromptu lecture. Because of the structure of interaction within these problem classes it was possible to increase their size to 24 and still manage to deal with students' individual queries.

The assessment was unchanged, involving an end-of-term exam. These costings therefore examine only the teaching input. They have been calculated for 72 students.

Original course (calculated for 72 students)	Staff time (hours)		Alternative course
Teaching			
Lectures (9 weeks x 4 hours)	36	9	Lectures (9 weeks x 1 hour)
Problem classes (9 weeks x 1hour x 4 groups of 18)	36	27	Problem classes (9 weeks x 1 hour x 3 groups of 24)
Total teaching hours	72	36	
Total teaching hours/student	1.00	0.50	
50% of former teaching costs			

This re-design cost half as much to teach. The effect on students was fascinating. Forced to work independently they did so - they had more time to do so as well. They turned up to problem classes much better prepared and were able to tackle more varied and advanced problems than previously. They became much more actively involved in the problem classes and sorted out many of their difficulties for each other. The lecturer was able to concentrate on interesting variations and more advanced applications rather than basics. It became clear that there was a great deal more co-operative learning taking place outside class time. The external examiner noted the improved quality of students' exam answers and the greater depth which was being achieved within the same syllabus.

There was a worry about student attendance. It was felt that some students might not turn up to the problem classes and that, without lectures, they would then perform very badly. A proportion of students did indeed not turn up and were hardly seen throughout the course. But most of these students actually performed better than those who turned up regularly! It seems that some students, provided they have clearly written material to work from, can learn Mathematics completely alone (as the Open University has proved). The new way of delivering the course suited these students and they performed well. A small proportion of students did not turn up even though they needed to and they performed badly. This seems to be the case with many courses which rely heavily on independent learning from packages. These students need careful monitoring and perhaps assessed coursework to keep them on track.

10.8 Education

The change in design of this course could be imitated by almost any theoretical Social Science or Education course. Lectures and tutor-led seminars were replaced by workshops and an independent seminar, supported by learning packages. The assessment was radically changed. Essays and an exam were replaced by multiple choice question tests, seminar presentations and a portfolio. Total teaching and assessment time was halved, allowing an increase in the number of students, while the quality of the learning improved and students' evaluation of the course improved markedly.

The original course, a Psychology of Learning two-term programme for Education students, was a "survey" course introducing the range of psychological approaches to the understanding of learning: behavioural, cognitive and so on. Material was presented in two lectures a week and followed up by a small-group session in which a student presented a seminar. Students submitted two essays, one each term, and sat a two-hour exam at the end of the course.

The quality of the seminars was already a cause for concern and an increase in student numbers made it inevitable that seminar size would have to be drastically increased. Students were becoming disengaged as the course grew in size and essays and exam papers revealed a lack of breadth of coverage, with students consistently avoiding some theoretical approaches or showing poor understanding of them.

The re-design had the following features:

- The course was re-structured around the six theoretical approaches, allocating a three-week "unit" to each approach.

- Each unit was supported by a specially written learning package, which contained a detailed programme of the sessions, explanatory material, practical exercises or small projects, and a detailed bibliography. Each unit involved a short independent individual or group project.

- Each week's teaching consisted of a three-hour session. The first and third hours took place in a large flat-floored room and took the form of workshops involving substantial individual and group work interspersed with short presentations by the tutor - like very interactive lectures.

- The middle hour involved students in autonomous seminar groups meeting in separate rooms. In each group a pair of students presented a seminar which was peer-assessed against four clear criteria. Each pair gave two such seminar presentations during the course and the assessment counted for 20% of the course marks. Two tutors toured the six parallel groups to monitor their operation, sitting and joining in where appropriate.

- Each of the units was assessed by a multiple choice question test administered during the third hour of the third week of the unit. These tests were computer-marked and the results handed back the next week. These six tests counted for 30% of the marks for the course.

- The seminar and MCQ assessment ensured that students took all of the course more seriously and did not selectively neglect what they disliked. The written work - the essays and exam - were replaced by a portfolio in which students had to present accounts of four workshops, four seminars and four projects. This required more constant attention throughout the course. The portfolio was created and discussed as students worked through the course.

The costings have been calculated for the number of students the new course had to cope with: 72.

Original course (calculated for 72 students)	Staff time (hours)		Course in 1990
Teaching			
Lectures (18 weeks x 2 hours)	36	36	Workshops (18 weeks x 2 hours)
Seminars (18 weeks x 9 groups of 8)	162	36	Autonomous seminars (18 weeks x 2 "touring" tutors, x 6 groups of 12)
Total teaching hours	198	72	
Total teaching hours/student	2.75	1.00	
36% of former teaching costs			
Assessment			
Essays (72 x 2 at 20 mins)	48		
Exam (72 x 2 questions at 10 mins)	24		
		6	6 x MCQ tests (at 1 hour per test)
		18	Seminar presentations (36 pairs x 2 seminars, 1hour per week collation)
		36	Portfolio (72 at 30 mins)
Total assessment hours	72	60	
Total assessment hours/student	1.00	0.83	
83% of former assessment costs			
Total staffing hours	270	132	
Total staffing hours/student	3.75	1.83	
49% of former total staffing costs			

The seminars worked far better than when they were run by tutors. Students prepared better, gave clearer presentations, often supported by handouts and references, and those not presenting joined in more more readily even though the groups were 50% larger. This was due partly to the assessment of the seminar presentations by peers, who were intolerant of poorly run seminars, and partly to the fact that students were much less inhibited when the tutor was out of the room. Tutors had to learn to keep a low profile when they joined groups.

Students worked fairly well between the workshop sessions, allowing the session to be used to process the data collected or discuss reading undertaken in the projects between sessions. Students initially performed poorly in the multiple choice question tests. They assumed that they would be easy, but discovered that they really needed to understand the theories to answer the questions. The portfolio idea supported the course well in that students needed to attend and participate in sessions to collect the necessary material, and to work steadily throughout the course. The portfolios themselves became a little bulky, however, and were difficult to mark in the absence of clear criteria and experience in marking this kind of product.

Student evaluation of the course was overwhelmingly positive, with every innovation being preferred to its conventional alternative by a clear majority of students.

The re-design of the course required considerable investment. As well as the total re-casting of the course, the six learning packages and six MCQ tests needed to be written and the tutors had to learn how to handle large workshop sessions. The initial design and writing work was funded through 80 hours of part-time lecturer support. This investment was more than recovered in the first year of operation and as the course ran for six years largely without change the investment was very worthwhile.

11 Course re-design costing sheet

Current course No. of students......	**Staff time (hours)**	**Future course** No. of students ......
Teaching		
Total teaching hours Total teaching hours/student		
Assessment		
Total assessment hours Total assessment hours/student		
Total staffing hours Total staffing hours/student		
Overall saving per student ....%		

Bibliography

Andresen, L.W. (1988), Lecturing to Large Groups: A Guide to Doing it Less...But Better. Kensington: Tertiary Education Research Centre, University of New South Wales

Andresen, L., Nightingale, P., Boud, D., and Magin, D. (1989), Strategies for Assessing Students, Teaching with Reduced Resources, no. 1. Kensington: Professional Development Centre, University of New South Wales

Educational Development Unit (1986), Ways of Reducing Teaching Contact Time. Perth: Educational Development Unit, Curtin University

Gibbs, G., Habeshaw, S., and Habeshaw, T. (1992), 53 Interesting Ways to Teach Large Classes. Bristol: Technical and Educational Services

Jaques, D., Gibbs, G., and Rust, C. (1991), Designing and Evaluating Courses. Oxford: Educational Methods Unit, Oxford Polytechnic

Jenkins, A., and Gibbs, G. (1992), Teaching Large Classes. London: Kogan Page

McGee, R. (1986), Teaching the Mass Class. American Sociological Association. Purdue University

Magin, D., Nightingale, P., Andresen, L., and Boud, D. (1989), Strategies for Increasing Students' Independence. Teaching with Reduced Resources, no. 2. Kensington: Professional Development Centre, University of New South Wales

Rowntree, D. (1985), Developing Courses for Students. New York: Harper & Row

Weimer, M.G. (ed.) (1987), Teaching Large Classes Well. London: Jossey-Bass